HOMES
Around the World

by Ellen Lawrence

Ruby Tuesday Books

Published in 2026 by Ruby Tuesday Books Ltd.

Copyright © 2026 Ruby Tuesday Books Ltd.

All rights reserved. No part of this publication may be reproduced in whole or in part, stored in any retrieval system, or transmitted in any form or by any means, electronic, mechanical, photocopying, recording, or otherwise, without written permission from the publisher.

Editor: Mark J. Sachner
Designer: Tammy West
Production: John Lingham & Tammy West

Photo credits:
Alamy: 4R (Paul Springett), 5T (Ariadne Van Zandbergen), 6T, 7 (Eric Lafforgue), 8T (Yaacov Shein), 16R (Thomas Cockrem), 16B (Friedrich Stark), 17 (Stephen Coyne); Corbis: 14; FLPA: 4; Istockphoto: 9, 18–19; Shutterstock: Cover (GuoZhongHua), 5BL (Jaren Jai Wicklund), 5BR (Yu Zhang), 6B (Andreas Fink), 8B (Kowit Sitthi), 10–11 (Pavel Svoboda Photography), 12L (Hung Chung Chih), 12T (Santhosh Varghese), 12B (Gudrun Hochmuth), 13 (leungchopan), 15 (kaetana), 18B (Maxim Petrichuk), 19T (Dmitry Chulov), 20 (Mohammad Bash), 21 (Orlok); Superstock: 4C.

Library of Congress Control Number: 2024949278
Hardback ISBN 978-1-78856-534-9
Paperback ISBN 978-1-78856-535-6
ePub ISBN 978-1-78856-536-3

Published in Minneapolis, MN
Printed in the United States

www.rubytuesdaybooks.com

The picture on the front cover of this book shows a floating home on Tonlé Sap Lake in Cambodia. Turn to page 8 to find out more about the people who live on the lake.

CONTENTS

Welcome to My Home 4

Building a Home 6

A Village on a Lake 8

Wooden Rainbow Houses 10

City Homes 12

Living in a City Slum 14

A Sumba Village 16

A Mongolian Tent Home 18

Leaving Your Home 20

Welcome to My World 22

Glossary 23

Index 24

Words shown in bold in the text are explained in the glossary.

All the places in this book are shown on the map on page 22.

Welcome to My Home

A home is a place to stay cool.

A home is a place to stay warm.

A home is a place to stay dry.

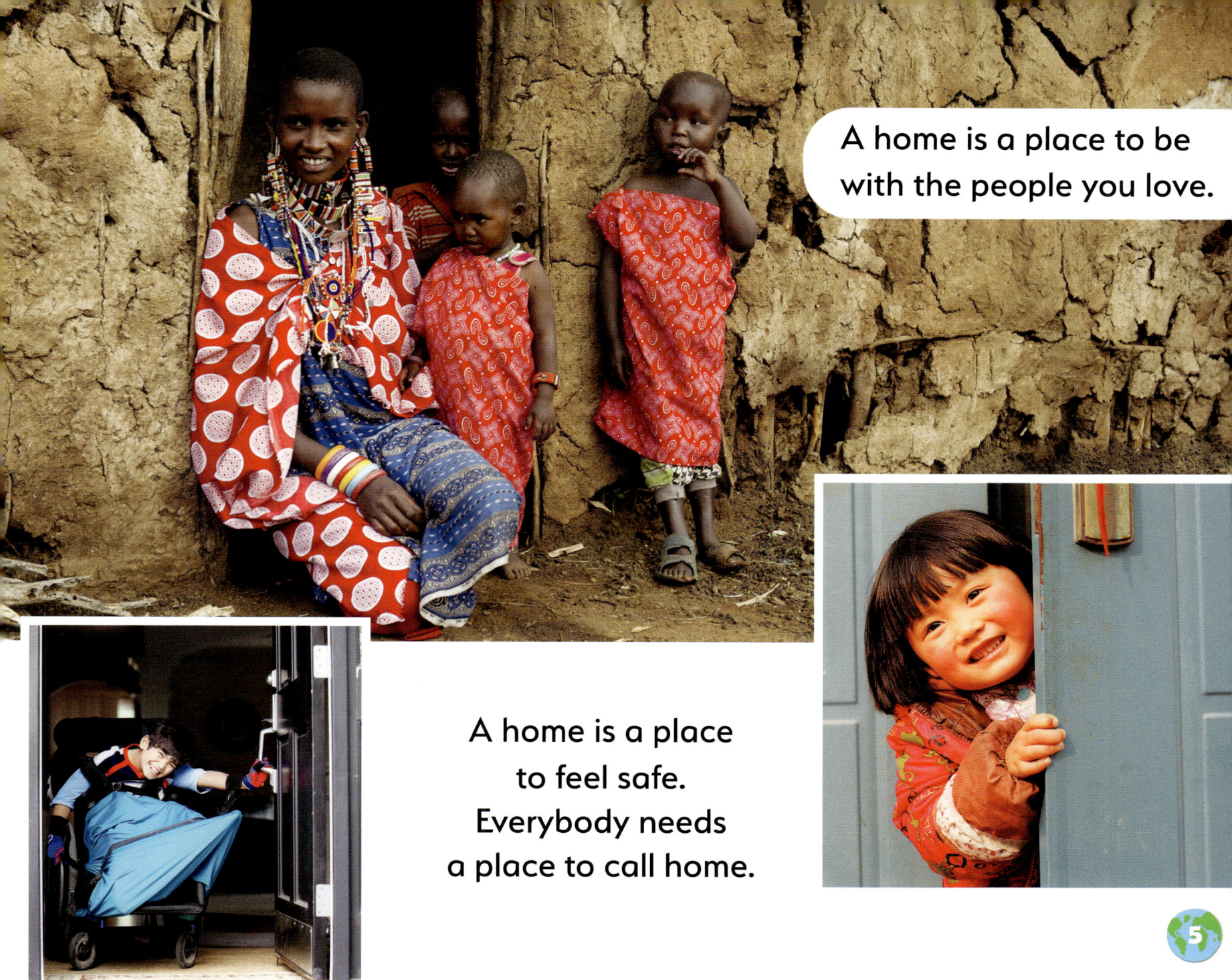

A home is a place to be with the people you love.

A home is a place to feel safe. Everybody needs a place to call home.

Building a Home

The Ovahimba people of Namibia live in small villages.

Sometimes they move from place to place to find grass for their goats and cattle.

Wherever they settle, Ovahimba people build small homes called **huts**.

Milking the goats

An Ovahimba hut

The huts are made of branches covered with dried mud and cow dung.

When Ovahimba children are very young, they live and sleep in a hut with their parents. Once they are about three years old, they share a hut with other children.

A Village on a Lake

On a huge lake in Cambodia, people live in floating villages.

The lake is called Tonlé Sap (TUHN-lay SAHP).

The children who live on the lake travel to their floating schools by boat.

A floating school

A floating food shop

A floating church

Some families make their homes in houses that float on the water.

Others live on houseboats.

The villages have floating gardens, gas stations, stores, and even floating basketball courts!

A house and garden

Wooden Rainbow Houses

On the tiny island of Kulusuk, the land turns white in winter. But there's still a rainbow of colors to be seen.

That's because everyone on Kulusuk lives in brightly painted wooden houses.

Kulusuk is just off the coast of Greenland.

The island is home to fewer than 300 people.

Lots of sled dogs live on Kulusuk.

They pull the sleds that people use to travel over the ice and snow.

Almost no trees grow in Greenland, so there's no wood for construction. All the pieces for a new house arrive by boat as a **kit**. Then the owners fit the pieces together to build their home.

City Homes

Around the world, billions of people live in big cities.

A city can be a noisy place with lots of traffic jams.

Many city homes do not have a garden or yard. People spend time outdoors in parks and playgrounds.

A crowded street in Kathmandu, in Nepal

City houses in San Francisco

Apartment blocks in Hong Kong

Many people in cities live in apartments high above the ground.

Living in a City Slum

Around the world, millions of very poor people make their homes in parts of cities known as **slums**.

They build small homes from materials they find on the streets and on garbage dumps.

The homes have no electricity, toilets, or water for drinking, cooking, and washing.

These children in a slum keep warm by burning garbage.

In Delhi, in India, thousands of families may share just one water tap in a slum area. Each day, adults and children stand in line for hours to fill buckets and plastic bottles with water from the tap.

A Sumba Village

On the Indonesian island of Sumba, people live in small villages.

In a village, there are large stone **monuments**.

Tombstone

They are the tombstones of villagers who have died throughout the centuries.

The people of Sumba raise pigs, water buffaloes, and chickens.

Water buffalo

The tower of a Sumba house is used as a safe place to keep precious objects. People believe that the **spirits** of their **ancestors** live in the towers of their homes.

The roof of a Sumba house is thatched with grasses.

Animals live in the bottom part of the house.

People live in this part of the house.

A Mongolian Tent Home

Many people in Mongolia are **nomads**.

They move from place to place to find fresh grass for their horses, camels, cattle, sheep, and goats.

They live in tent-like homes called gers.

A camel carrying a ger

A solar panel making electricity

A ger has a wooden frame. The frame may be covered with layers of felt made from sheep's wool. It also has an outer covering made from waterproof canvas.

Building a ger

It takes less than an hour to build or dismantle a ger!

Leaving Your Home

Every year, many people around the world have to leave their homes and become **refugees**.

Sometimes this happens because of a natural disaster such as a flood or earthquake.

Sometimes it's because of war.

Refugees may have to find safety in camps inside their own country or in neighboring countries.

People who become refugees may leave behind family, friends, and pets. Children have to leave behind their toys. There may be nowhere for them to go to school.

Many refugees live in a camp for years.

They hope that one day it will be safe to go home.

Children from Syria at a refugee camp

Welcome to My World

Canada
Page 4

Kulusuk, Greenland
Pages 10–11

England
Page 12

Syria
Pages 20–21

Nepal
Page 12

Mongolia
Pages 18–19

United States
Page 12

China
Page 5

United States
Page 5

India
Pages 14–15

Hong Kong, China
Page 13

Brazil
Page 4

Senegal
Page 4

Namibia
Pages 6–7

Kenya
Page 5

Cambodia
Pages 8–9

Sumba, Indonesia
Pages 16–17

North America

Europe

Asia

Africa

South America

Australia

22

GLOSSARY

ancestor
A relative who lived a long time ago. For example, your great-grandparents and great-great-grandparents are your ancestors.

hut
A small house that usually has just one room and one story.

kit
A collection of objects, such as pieces of wood, that can be fitted together to make something—for example, a piece of furniture or a complete house.

monument
A statue or other structure that is usually made of stone. A monument is made as a way to remember someone who has died, and it is often placed on a person's grave.

nomad
A person who regularly moves from one area to another and does not live in one place all the time.

refugee
A person who has been forced to leave their home to escape danger and needs to be protected.

slum
An overcrowded and often dirty area where many people live in poverty. A slum is usually in a city or on the edge of a city.

spirit
An invisible part of a person that many people believe lives on after death. For example, a ghost is a type of spirit.

INDEX

A
animals 6–7, 11, 16–17, 18, 20
apartments 13

C
Cambodia 8, 22
cities 12–13, 14–15

D
Delhi, India 14–15, 22

F
floating villages 8–9

G
gers 18–19

H
huts 6–7

K
Kulusuk, Greenland 10–11, 22

M
Mongolia 18–19, 22
monuments 16

N
Namibia 6, 22
nomads 18–19

O
Ovahimba people 6–7

R
refugees 20–21

S
slums 14–15
Sumba Island, Indonesia 16–17, 22
Syria 20–21, 22

T
Tonlé Sap lake 8–9